Myth Quest

Sarama and Sarameyas

THE HEAVENLY HOUNDS

retold by Anu Kumar

illustrations by Maya Magical Studios

First published in 2012 by Hachette India
(Registered name: Hachette Book Publishing India Pvt. Ltd)
An Hachette UK company
www.hachetteindia.com

SRD

ISBN 978-93-5009-325-2

Hachette Book Publishing India Pvt Ltd,
4th & 5th Floors, Corporate Centre;
Plot No. 94, Sector 44; Gurgaon 122003, India

Typeset in Adobe Garamond Pro 13/16
by Eleven Arts, New Delhi

Printed and bound in India by
Manipal Technologies Limited, Manipal

Welcome to the world of MythQuest . . .

Discover the fables and legends about the origin, history, deities, ancestors and heroes of India.

While the term 'myth' in common conversation means a false story, in the world of religion, folklore and magic, myths are considered 'true'. They tell stories of the creation of the universe, the eternal battle between good and evil and the history of humankind itself.

The main characters in our myths are bigger and better than any modern superheroes. They are birds and beasts, gods and demons, kings and queens, generals and warriors, sages and gurus, each with extraordinary powers that changed the course of history and the fate of the human race.

The people to whom a myth belongs consider it a true account of their past millions of years ago. Even today, they continue to worship the gods and goddesses, follow the rituals and read the texts that developed from these myths.

Hachette India's MythQuest series brings to you fascinating stories from the vast treasures of ancient mythology. Read them all—and become a MythMaster!

Mythological characters and events have been described in different ways in different versions of ancient texts. We have chosen the most interesting and key stories to build a comprehensive account for the young reader.

This story is about . . .

*Sarama, or the Hound of Heaven, and her children known as the Sarameyas. The name Sarama means 'the fleet-footed one'. In the Rig Veda, there are two words that describe her—*supadi*, which means fair-footed or quick, and* subhaga*, or the fortunate one, who is loved by all. Sarama was a celestial dog, and belonged to Indra, the King of Gods and Lord of Heaven. She was also called* devashuni*, or beloved of the gods.*

No one really knows of her origins. She is sometimes believed to be one of the daughters of King Daksha, a great king and demigod born from the mind of Brahma, the God of Creation. While some texts say that she was the mother of the entire race of dogs, others believe that she was the mother of all wild animals including tigers and lions. In the early Vedas, Sarama is depicted not as a dog, but as a lovely, fair-footed goddess. Some other stories mention that Sarama is the sister of Brihaspati, the great spiritual teacher of the gods.

As the mother of all dogs, Sarama was the first of her kind and she gave birth to great dogs known as the Sarameyas. Two of the first Sarameyas were named Shyama and Sabala, and were the four-eyed magnificent creatures who went on to serve Yama, the God of Death.

Here is their tale full of barks of bravery . . .

CHAPTER ONE

THE GREAT CATTLE THEFT

This story takes place a long, long time ago when human beings were pastoral nomads and belonged to different tribes. Our story is about the most ancient of these tribes known as the Angirasas. They were named after the powerful sage called Angiras as they were believed to be his descendents. They had huge herds of cattle and were peaceful nomads who moved across the world in search of new pastures. Their journeys often covered great distances and took them to many wondrous lands.

Once, during a search for good grazing land, they wandered into an area which was home to a tribe

known as the Panis. Now the Panis were very different from the Angirasas and were among the most feared peoples in the ancient world. They were aggressive, warlike and as fierce as demons. They had no cattle of their own and lived off the spoils of loot and plunder. They stayed in huge walled mud forts, beside a wide river called Rasa, and travelled far and wide, pillaging other lands.

This was the land that the Angirasas unknowingly wandered into and decided to set up their camp. When night fell, it was darker than any other. The clouds swarmed in thick and fast and covered all traces of the moon and stars from the sky. The Angirasas shivered with fear because these simple pastoral folk feared the dark. To them darkness stood for everything that was unknown and fearsome. And they prayed to Ushas, Goddess of Dawn, and praised the sun and the power of light. That night, however, there was no respite from the dark. They tethered their animals to their posts and retired to their tents to sleep through this deadly blackness. Exhausted and afraid, they finally fell asleep.

As the Angirasas slept in their tents, and the wild animals and spirits roamed freely everywhere, someone crept into their camp and stole the large herds of cattle that the tribe owned. It was done so stealthily that the sleeping nomads continued to slumber. Their guards were asleep, heads lolling on their chests, and that was how they were found the next morning.

When day broke and the sun's rays chased away the thick black threads of night, the Angirasas received a great shock. They headed for their cattle pens like they did every single day to take the animals out to graze. However, as thay neared the enclosure, they were struck by the fact that there was unearthly silence. There was not a squeak from the cattle pens, and the gates were wide open, the guards asleep and not one single cow stood in the enclosures! They also saw their makeshift wooden fences broken in places. And there was not a single sign of the hundreds of cows that had been there just the night before!

Some of the Angirasas began wailing in distress for their lives depended on their cattle. Some others sprang into action and immediately set out on their horses, hoping they would catch sight of the animals. They rode out in different directions, but the grasslands stretched as far as the eye could see without a trace of any living thing. Some of the Angirasas clambered up a hillock to get a better view. They could see forests nearby and a little further away, there were some hills with the ramparts of mud forts. Now the Angirasas had heard of the Panis and their mud forts and quickly realized that this was their land.

When the riders returned to the camp, they described what they had seen. Some of their elders were immediately suspicious of the Panis. They knew that the Panis were aggressive and would make life difficult for anyone who encroached on their land. The peaceful Angirasas did not quite understand the Panis and were afraid of their violent ways. They knew they would not be able to deal with them on their own and so they turned to Indra, the King of Gods. Only he could help them get back their lost cattle and so they earnestly prayed to Lord Indra for his help.

CHAPTER TWO

THE DISLOYAL EAGLE

On hearing the Angirasas' pleas, Indra appeared before them and heard them out. He was the most powerful of all gods and they knew he would help them in their plight. He was the god who created rains, which in turn made the grasslands green and fed all the cattle in the world, and the Angirasas lived for their cattle. They were also Lord Indra's loyal devotees who worshipped him through the year, so he could not refuse them. He closed his eyes and thought of Suparna, the magnificent bird. In a heartbeat, the skies turned blue and black as the magnificent Suparna appeared, beating his huge and powerful wings.

Suparna was an eagle who had supernatural powers.

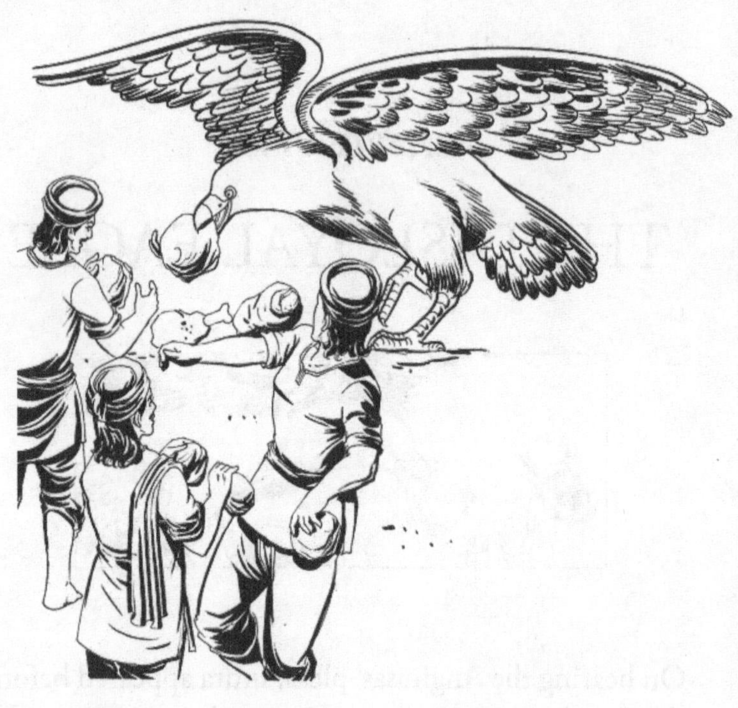

He had eyes that could pick up the tiniest of objects from a long distance away, and he flew faster than any other bird.

As Suparna flew over the mud forts of the Panis to see if they had indeed stolen the cows, he was spotted by their lookouts. As the great eagle swooped down, the Panis bribed him into silence with chunks of succulent meat. Despite being a divine creature, Suparna could not control his greed and having eaten his fill, he flew back to Heaven, and told Indra that he had seen no sign of the Angirasas' cattle. 'I think there is some magic at work here and they have just disappeared into thin air,' said Suparna.

The Angirasas were deeply disappointed. They looked at Lord Indra with tears in their eyes, not knowing what they would do next. Now Lord Indra could tell that Suparna was lying, and for this, he was punished. The great eagle was banished from Heaven and sent to roam the earth and fend for himself. From that day on, he and his descendents had to rely on the power of their eyes to hunt for prey and survive. The joys of Heaven were lost to them for ever.

Lord Indra had sent Suparna to investigate, but he had failed him. As the Angirasas grew even more despondent, Indra realized that he would have to do something quickly to mend the situation. The Angirasas were afraid that the mysterious cattle thieves would never be apprehended. Although they suspected the Panis, there was not a shred of evidence to prove it.

CHAPTER THREE

SARAMA COMES TO THE RESCUE

Despite much thought, Lord Indra still couldn't come up with a suitable solution and he decided to turn to his guru, Brihaspati, for help. Now Brihaspati was a very wise and all-knowing sage and Indra always went to him for help when he was in a difficult situation.

When Brihaspati heard what the matter was, he closed his eyes to meditate. After a short while he opened them and provided a simple solution. 'You must send Sarama,' he pronounced. 'She is perfect for this job. She has been a most faithful companion to all the gods. Her powerful sense of smell has warded off many a danger and her sharp ears have heard your enemies' footfalls long before they approached. She will be able to help you find the cattle.'

Sarama, the divine hound, was indeed beloved of the gods. Her powerful senses had made her invaluable to Heaven in times of war and danger. The gods trusted her intuition and powers of deduction, because of which she was also often the chosen messenger of the gods.

Sarama had also been blessed by the sage Brihaspati because she was an honourable and devoted creature who never veered from the path of truth and goodness. Unlike the magnificent bird Suparna, who had given in to temptation, Sarama was known to be steadfast, loyal and dependable.

Lord Indra followed his guru's advice and immediately sent for Sarama. She soon trotted up and bowed low before her master. Indra told her what she must do, and promised to reward her handsomely if she returned with good news.

'Do you swear to that, O King of Heaven? Will you reward me if I make every effort to find the lost cattle of the Angirasas?' Sarama asked, her forelegs stretched before the King of Gods, her head bowed low.

'I will grant you anything you desire,' Lord Indra replied. As sunlight reflected off his golden crown and filled Heaven with a wonderful light, Sarama was awestruck by her master's glory and ready to do anything for him.

Now Sarama knew the Panis were dangerous and there was every chance that she would not return alive. Yet, Indra's offer was tempting as he had promised to reward her with whatever she wanted. Also, he was her favourite god and so Sarama quickly made up her mind.

'I will do as you ask,' she said. 'But it is a dangerous mission and I might not return alive. All I want is a small favour from you. Please look after my descendents. May they always have milk and food, may they have shelter and lead comfortable lives and never know starvation. That is all I desire.'

Although Sarama's speech would sound like woofs to any normal ear, to Lord Indra, her words were crystal clear. The King of Gods nodded his head and raised his hand in acknowledgement. 'Your wish shall be granted,' he said.

So Sarama set off on a long and perilous journey to recover the lost cattle. Lord Indra followed her on his magnificent white elephant, Airavata. Sarama crossed a large river and then broke into a fast run, for she had picked up a scent. It was a quiet morning and Sarama ran for a long while, her nose close to the ground, sniffing hard as she sped across the land. At times she trotted, then she would slow down to pick up the scent. Suddenly, she would pick up speed again till she was nearly galloping. Far behind, came Lord Indra on Airavata.

Sometimes she waited for him to catch up, and then raised her head slowly, taking in the air. Then she was off again, running faster than anything Indra had ever known before, swifter than any other creature he had seen. He watched her follow the smell through the forests, across streams and over the hills. Even Lord Indra had a hard time following her. Behind him came the other gods and the Angirasas. Sarama ran hard, her panting loud in the stillness of the jungle. Finally she stopped at a stone cave in the middle of the forest. This was an ancient cave called Vala, where the Panis often rested while out on hunts.

The moment Sarama stopped in front of Vala, everyone's suspicions about the Panis were confirmed.

Lord Indra had spotted the cave from a distance and realized that the Panis were up to no good. What Suparna had failed to do, the loyal Sarama had achieved.

However, her work was far from over and the most dangerous part of her journey still remained. Now she would have to go in and retrieve the cattle from the thieves.

Lord Indra had spotted the cattle from a distance and realized the Panis were up to no good. What [illegible] had failed to do, the loyal Sarama had achieved.

However, her work was far from over and the most laborious part of her journey still remained. Now she would have to go back and lead the cattle from the [illegible].

CHAPTER FOUR

SARAMA'S BRAVERY

Sarama paused to catch her breath as she reached the mouth of Vala. With her acute sense of smell, she had followed the trail of the cattle thieves and ended up at this cave. She knew that both the cattle and the thieves were inside the cave. She also knew that it could only be the Panis and they were extremely dangerous. Yet, without a care for her own safety, she raised her hackles and started barking loudly, calling out to the men safely hidden inside the cave.

Some of the Panis finally emerged. On seeing a mere dog at the entrance, they laughed. 'Is this the best champion the Angirasas could find?' they said dismissively. Some of them even tried to scare Sarama away by throwing small pebbles at her.

However, Sarama was brave and not one to be threatened by insults. She dodged the flying missiles, raised her head and inched towards them growling menacingly. 'Release the stolen animals. You have taken them unlawfully and now you must return them,' she said with a growl.

Then she started barking so loudly that the sound echoed through the forest and the large cave. The Panis who had been laughing till a moment ago, now began to get nervous. Some of them even retreated into the cave while the leaders tried to warn her off.

'Be off, you stupid hound,' they snarled. 'We know that you are a favoured creature of the gods, yet that will not save you. Don't try and mess with us. We are well-armed and will not yield the cows without battle,' they said. 'You alone are hardly capable of standing against our whole tribe.'

One proud Pani leader walked towards her and said, 'The cows you are looking for are well hidden in a rocky chamber deep inside this cave and only one of us can get them out. Take this information to your leaders, as there is little else that you can do, however divine and special you might be.'

Now although the Panis were generally dismissive of the gods, they had realized that mere strength would not help them gain power in the world. They knew

that they needed the gods on their side and the cows had been stolen for that specific purpose. The Panis wanted the cows for the butter and milk they would produce. This in turn would enable them to conduct special sacrifices to please the three all-powerful gods, Brahma, Vishnu and Shiva. They believed that once the divine trinity was pleased, they would grant the Panis all that they desired and enable them to rule over the world and all the other tribes. The power-hungry Panis wanted nothing more than to become masters of all the worlds and even Heaven if it was possible.

Sarama, with her intuitive powers, immediately understood what their plan was and realized that the cattle needed to be retrieved at all cost.

She was unyielding and stood her ground in the face of all their threats and their vast numbers. She bared her teeth in a most menacing manner. 'No matter how much you threaten me, you are lost creatures,' she said. 'Your plan will never materialize and in a short time you will come face to face with the combined army of Lord Indra and his gods, as well as the large masses of furious Angirasas whose livelihood you have stolen away in such a cowardly manner.'

Thus Sarama and the leaders of the Panis stood face to face at the mouth of the cave, neither side yielding or moving back. Now the Panis were a cunning lot. When they realized that Sarama was nothing like Suparna and that she was a favoured creature of Indra, they decided to change tactics. Their spies had told them about Indra's promise to Sarama, and they decided to match the god's offer and tempt Sarama with all kinds of good things.

'Now there is no need to get so aggressive,' said the Panis. 'You are like one of us, sister Sarama. You are brave and strong and you could live with us and be one of us. Why bother going back to a slave's life in Heaven when we can give you all kinds of comfort and luxury right here? You can eat all that you want. And we will even ensure that you have fresh milk from these Angirasa cows every single day.'

These bribes had no effect on Sarama and she just growled dangerously at each word. Then something strange happened. Sarama's eyes first turned green and then a fiery red in the darkness. The Panis moved backwards for it was quite a terrifying sight and they believed that it was evil magic at work. What they didn't know was that Lord Agni, the God of Fire, had accompanied Sarama in an invisible form to help light her way in the dark places that she would encounter along her journey. It was Lord Agni who gave her these powers to back her up.

With her eyes blazing, she reared up on her hind legs and snarled a clear 'No' to all their offers. The Panis were truly frightened at this and most of them took a good many steps away from her.

Yet, a few remaining men still persisted. 'If you stay with us, you will never know a hungry day in your life,' they said. 'You and your descendents will never have to go hunting in the forests and we will look after them as well. Whatever we have, our cattle, our riches, are yours too. We will willingly share everything with you.'

But Sarama stared back fiercely and answered, 'Return the cattle at once, for you are trapped in this cave. Outside, Lord Indra waits with his vast army of gods, and you do not stand a chance. It is best you surrender the stolen cattle of the Angirasas and beg for forgiveness.'

However, the Panis were as proud as they were conniving and refused to budge, or give up. They retreated into their cave and emerged with a huge army of men. Seeing this, Sarama returned to Lord Indra, who began preparing his troops for battle. Although the Panis were strong, they were no match for Indra and his heavenly army backed up by the Angirasas. The Panis were completely outnumbered in the battle that ensued and decisively defeated. The cattle was finally retrieved as Indra destroyed the gigantic cave of Vala with a mighty blow of his weapon, the all-powerful Vajra.

And as the cattle left the cave, and the Panis stood around, their heads low in defeat, the waters of seven rivers came gushing down from Heaven and flowed down into the earth. So the land prospered and the Angirasas lived long, happy lives and the world was saved from the evil plans of the Panis. The cattle had been freed with Sarama's help and she in turn was responsible for the prosperous time on earth that followed.

In another version of the story, it was Sarama who found the first divine cows and taught the first human beings on earth to domesticate them, milk them and use the milk for various other preparations like butter and ghee. As a helper and loyal friend of humans, it is Sarama who prayed to the gods and implored Heaven to release the seven rivers onto earth, and bring an end to all the drought and suffering faced by man.

Both Sarama and her children came to the help of gods and men whenever they were called upon. To this day, Sarameyas are regarded as symbols of loyalty and devotion.

CHAPTER FIVE

THE STORY OF THE FIRST SARAMEYAS

The two Sarameyas born of Sarama were also blessed with divine powers and were called Shyama and Sabala. They were two very special dogs with four eyes and streaked golden coats. Once they grew up, they went on to serve as messengers of Yama, the God of Death and Dharma. These Sarameyas served as guardians on the road to Heaven, guiding souls who had passed on from earth through the rocky paths of Hell, into the golden portals of Heaven.

As they were messengers of the God of Death, they had a fearsome appearance, but their job was

to protect and guide dead souls. Day after day, Lord Yama would send his two dogs to search out all the men who were ready to join their forebears in Heaven.

There is another story about the origin of the first Sarameyas. A long time ago there were two *asuras* called Kalakanjas, who were fierce in countenance and cruel by nature. They once performed a terrible sacrifice to control Heaven and killed humans and other creatures and built a huge altar with their carcasses.

The gods were frightened and shocked at the cruelty of the *asuras* and begged Lord Indra to help them. Lord Indra disguised himself as a dead body and turned into a part of the altar.

Once the *asuras* completed the rituals of the sacrifice, they used their altar as steps by which they could climb up to Heaven. As they neared the heavenly portal, Lord Indra dropped himself out of the pile, and as a result the whole altar tumbled down along with the *asuras*. The dead bodies that crashed down to earth became spiders. However, two of these spiders flew up

to Heaven and were blessed by the gods. They became the heavenly dogs—Shyama and Sabala.

Apart from Shyama and Sabala, their descendents were also favoured by the gods and well looked after, in keeping with Lord Indra's promise to Sarama.

Once in Ayodhya, during the rule of Lord Rama when everything was peaceful and just, a dog came to the great king's court with a complaint.

'What is your problem, O Sarameya', said Rama gently. The dog was a poor bedraggled creature who bore marks of a beating all over his body.

'I was beaten by a Brahmin for no reason at all,' said the dog.

On hearing this, Rama summoned the Brahmin for questioning and coming face to face with the great king, the Brahmin confessed his crime. 'I was hungry and roaming the land, begging for alms and this dog just came into my path and blocked my way,' said the Brahmin. 'I told him to move, but he ignored my command. I was annoyed at this insolence from a mere dog, so I beat him with my stick.'

As Rama was a fair king, he punished the Brahmin and sent him away to undertake a penance for his crime and the dog was awarded the justice that was due to him.

Another story in the Mahabharata describes how those who were cruel to Sarama's children usually came to a sticky end, irrespective of whether they were kings, priests, or warriors. Janamejaya is one such king who was cursed because of his cruelty to a Sarameya.

CHAPTER SIX

SARAMA'S CURSE

King Janamejaya was the great-grandson of the Pandava prince Arjuna, and ruler of Hastinapura. Once his brothers were out on a hunt and were galloping through the woods, when a dog wandered into their path. They gave the dog a good beating for no fault of its own and sent it scurrying away. The poor, injured dog whimpered in pain and limped his way to his mother, Sarama. 'I did nothing wrong!' he said. 'I neither jumped at them, nor licked them, nor did I try to get at their things.'

Sarama tried to comfort him the best she could and then she made her way to Janamejaya and angrily cursed him saying, 'This son of mine did nothing wrong! Why was he beaten? Just as your family harmed him for doing no wrong, similarly a great danger will befall you due to no fault of yours.'

Janamejaya tried to defend his actions but he knew that his brothers were at fault and they had injured the dog merely for sport.

Sarama refused to be mollified and repeated her terrible curse. 'Your brothers harmed my son for no reason, and so my curse stands,' she said. 'Some unseen danger will befall you, and the sacrifice that you have set your heart on will never be fulfilled.'

The curse frightened the king. He had a really important sacrifice coming up where all the snakes in

the world would burn to death if all went well. This was to avenge the death of his father, Parikshit, at the hands of the snake-king Takshak.

Now Parikshit had accidentally disturbed a sage while he was in deep meditation and in return the sage had cursed him saying that he would be bitten by Takshak. True enough, when the time came, Parikshit was bitten by Takshak and died. Since then, Janamejaya had sworn vengeance against the *nagas*, or serpents and had planned his great sacrifice which would destroy all the snakes in the world.

However, now Janamejaya had been cursed and in order to salvage his great *yagna*, or sacrifice, the king searched throughout the kingdom till he found the great priest called Somashravas, and pleaded with him to lift Sarama's curse.

But Somashravas knew that this was well nigh impossible. Sarama was a truthful and loyal dog and her curse had great powers. The sacrifice itself was very complicated, but if it was conducted in the proper manner without any interruptions, the snakes thus summoned by the power of the mantras, would become absolutely powerless, fall into the sacrificial fire and die despite a curse.

King Janamejaya had made all the arrangements for this sacrifice and even appointed an official called Lohitaksha to check the dimensions of the hall and sacrificial altar. However, despite the fact that everything was built according to plan, Lohitaksha had grievous reservations. 'O King, I have measured everything and despite being mathematically accurate, I can see ill-omens at work which foretell that this sacrifice shall be interrupted due to the intervention of a priest.'

And King Janamejaya at once recalled Sarama's curse. He grew worried, but time was of the essence, and the priests warned that the auspicious hour would soon be over if the sacrifice didn't commence soon. So the king gave orders to his guards that no one was to be let into the sacrificial hall without his permission.

The great sacrifice began. The priests were clad in black, for this was a sacrifice directed towards destruction. As they chanted the appropriate verses, snakes, drawn by the power of these incantations, started converging from all over the universe.

There were snakes of all shapes and sizes and as the priests called each snake by name and uttered a mantra, it would immediately jump into the fire and die.

The sacrifice went on for days on end. Snakes perished in thousands in the huge fire. At this point, a priest called Astika came to visit the palace. The sacrifice was now nearing completion and the king welcomed his new guest and asked if there was anything he wanted. For one of the rules of a great sacrifice is that the king offers gifts to priests, sages and other men of learning.

But the chief priest intervened, 'O King, the sacrifice is not yet complete. Takshak, whose destruction you desired, is still alive. Wait till he is in the fire, before you begin giving gifts to any one.'

Janamejaya was puzzled and displeased at once. 'Why is Takshak still alive? Invoke the mantra with his name and make him fall into the fire.'

The priests uttered the appropriate verses, but nothing happened. They studied the omens and used their powers to interpret the cause. Finally, the head priest said, 'O King, Takshak has sought Lord Indra's protection and the King of Gods is safeguarding him in his own palace in Heaven and that is why our verses have not worked.'

The king was insistent, hounded by the fear that Sarama's curse might come true. 'Then utter the mantra in such a manner,' he ordered, 'that Takshak is impelled to fall into this fire, despite Indra's protection.'

The chief priest chanted a very powerful verse that ended with the ominous words, 'May Takshak fall into this fire and if Lord Indra continues to protect him, may he follow his loyal devotee.'

Such was the power of this mantra that both Lord Indra and Takshak started falling into the sacrificial fire, bound to each other. When Lord Indra saw that his friend's fate was inevitable and that nothing could save him, he decided to let go of Takshak and save himself. Takshak started descending helplessly, drawn towards the fire.

At this moment, Astika raised his hand and uttered some magic words and halted Takshak's fall. He then turned to Janamejaya and said, 'This is the gift you must make me, O powerful king. Please halt the sacrifice at this juncture. You have already killed millions of snakes in revenge for your father's death. I am a priest, and my mother is Jaratkaru, who is the sister of Vasuki, the foremost of the serpents. She sent me here to stop your sacrifice and to save her kinsmen.'

King Janamejaya hesitated. At this point the great sage Vyasa spoke to him, and advised him to grant

Astika's request. Thus advised by the sage for whom he had great respect, the king gave orders for the sacrifice to end. Sarama's curse came true and ever since, Janamejaya ensured that he and everyone else in his kingdom treated all the Sarameyas with great love and respect.

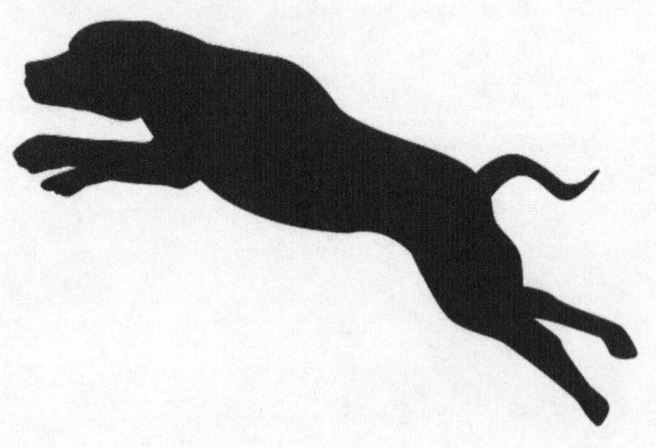

CHAPTER SEVEN

A LOYAL SARAMEYA AND A RIGHTEOUS KING

Another famous story about the Sarameyas was that of the faithful dog who accompanied Yudhishthira to Heaven.

Long after the battle of Mahabharata and after Yudhishthira had ruled over Hastinapura for many years, he and the other Pandavas—Arjuna, Bhima, Nakula and Sahadeva—as well as Draupadi resolved to retire from the world. So the Pandava brothers gave everything up, crowned Arjuna's grandson Parikshit as

king and set off on the long journey. First, they started moving eastwards when all of a sudden, a dog appeared along the path and started following them. Very soon, it became part of their group and accompanied them to different parts of the world. First, they went to a great ocean where Arjuna relinquished his famous bows and arrows that had won him great victories. Then they went south and the dog followed. Then they went north and the dog still followed. As they crossed the mighty Himalayas and the cold deserts and scaled the unbelievable heights of Mount Meru, the dog continued with them, braving all the elements, the cruel weather and the extremely harsh and difficult terrain. Draupadi was the first to fall. Then the younger Pandavas fell one by one, all except Yudhishthira.

This eldest son of Pandu did not once turn back. Unfazed by the circumstances he walked on. And all through he was followed by the Sarameya that had kept him company on the long and arduous journey.

At long last, after the two of them, man and dog had walked a long while, Lord Indra arrived in his wonderful chariot to take Yudhishthira to Heaven. 'You have earned your place in Heaven,' said Lord Indra. 'Get into my chariot and come take your rightful place.'

When Yudhishthira made a move to get on to the chariot with the dog, Indra stopped him saying, 'Only you can come. You are going to be blessed with the gifts of the gods and this dog surely cannot accompany you to such a magnificent place.' However, the gentle and righteous Yudhishthira refused to part with his faithful companion.

'This dog, O Lord of Heaven, has proved himself to be very devoted to me. He must accompany me wherever you take me. This son of Sarama has followed me through wind and rain, through heat and dust, and through the cruellest of thirst and worst of hunger. It has not fallen back or complained and has given me the strength to go on when I felt I was weak and ready to drop down,' said Yudhishthira.

Lord Indra patted him gently and said, 'You foolish king, you are giving up the wealth of Heaven for this lowly animal. Leave him behind and it will not affect your reputation as an honourable and great king.'

But no matter how hard Lord Indra tried to dissuade him, Yudhishthira remained adamant. He said, 'I do not desire the happiness of Heaven if I have to cast off a creature so devoted to me. Abandoning someone this loyal—a true devotee, is sin indeed.'

'There are certain rules in Heaven,' said Lord Indra. 'These are enforced by the deities called Krodhavasas. All humans who enter Heaven with animals are punished. All their good deeds on earth are forgotten and they are given a lowly place. Abandon this dog now and you will get your rightful rewards.'

Yudhishthira however was insistent. 'I shall not abandon this dog even though it may cost me my happiness in the afterlife.'

Lord Indra then tried a different line of argument. 'You have already abandoned your brothers and Krishna. You have renounced everything else. Why can't you renounce this dog?'

Despite all of Lord Indra's arguments, Yudhishthira refused to give up the Sarameya, and replied: 'It is well known that there is neither friendship nor enmity with those that are dead. When my brothers and Krishna died, I was unable to bring them back from death. I was forced to abandon them, and accept their death. I did not, however, abandon them as long as they were alive. To leave someone who has sought your protection and been such a good friend is a great sin. I cannot bring myself to commit such a sin.'

Lord Indra finally gave up trying to persuade Yudhishthira as he was so adamant on sticking to his path and protecting the dog. At that very moment, the Sarameya transformed into Yama and blessed Yudhishthira.

'You are the true follower of Dharma—the rules that laid down what was right and what was wrong. You have cast off every argument and resisted all the temptation that Lord Indra offered for a mere dog. O King, there is no one in this world who is equal to you. You are indeed worthy of Heaven and its gates will always be open for you,' he said.

And thus Yudhishthira rode off to Heaven in Lord Indra's splendid chariot, where he was reunited with all his loved ones.

Since this incident, Sarama and her children were blessed by the gods and continue to be associated with Dharma, loyalty and steadfast devotion in spite of all odds.

"It is well known that there is neither friendship nor enmity with those that are dead. When my brothers and Draupadi died, I was unable to bring them back from death. I was forced to abandon them, and accept their death. I did not, however, abandon them as long as they were alive. To leave someone who has sought your protection and been such a good friend is a great sin. I cannot bring myself to commit such a sin."

Lord Indra finally gave up trying to persuade Yudhishthira as he was so adamant on sticking to his path and protecting the dog. [illegible] the [illegible] man from [illegible] Yudhishthira [illegible]

[illegible] the [illegible] bid down what [illegible] and what was wrong. You have cast me [illegible] and resisted all the temptation that [illegible] offered for [illegible] dog. O King, there is no one in this world who is equal to you. You are indeed worthy of Heaven and its gates will always be open for you," he said.

And thus Yudhishthira [illegible] Heaven in Lord Indra's [illegible] chariot, where he was reunited with all his loved ones.

[illegible] the mother Sarama and her children were blessed by the gods and continue to be associated with Dharma, loyalty and steadfast devotion in spite of all odds.

CHAPTER EIGHT

THE FAITHFUL SARAMEYAS OF THE GODS

Apart from upholding the sacred laws of Dharma, Sarama and her children were associated with a number of gods and were the favoured creatures as well as symbols for a good many of them. When Lord Shiva took on his fearsome Bhairava form, he was often accompanied by a Sarameya.

Shiva assumed the form of Bhairava to teach Lord Brahma a lesson. As Bhairava, or Kaal Bhairava, some of Lord Shiva's most fearsome aspects were revealed.

His ornaments were actually serpents draped around his limbs, and human bones made up the cloth he wore around himself. In this form he was accompanied by his faithful Sarameya called Shvan, and was often shown seated on Shvan as well.

Shiva took on this form when Lord Brahma's arrogance displeased him. Lord Brahma had once told Vishnu that as the Creator of the Universe, he deserved to be worshipped more than any other god in the trinity. Now Shiva overheard this conversation and was furious. In his fury, he assumed the Bhairava avatar and

as Bhairava, he beheaded one of Brahma's five heads. Since then Brahma has had four heads turned towards every direction of the universe.

In another story, Bhairava cuts off one of Brahma's five heads when the latter could not keep his eyes off Saraswati. The goddess was a deity he had created himself and she had appeared in the form of Shatarupa to ease the chaos that had resulted when the universe was being created. Shatarupa took on different forms to evade Brahma's gaze but the god soon got wise to this. Finally, it was Shiva who intervened in his Bhairava form and resolved to teach Brahma a lesson. When he cut off one of his heads, Brahma at once realized the futility of what he was doing and was repentant.

As Bhairava, Shiva visited cremation grounds and danced the *tandava* dance of destruction. His *vahana* was the black Shvan who was often seen accompanying his master in places that most other gods or humans fear to tread.

Lord Shiva in his other form as Rudra, or the one who roars in anger, also has a dog as his vehicle. Virabhadra, the divine creature formed out of the wrath of Shiva, in his Rudra avatar, is also depicted with a Sarameya. This great warrior has a serpent hood, carries a mace, a shield and a severed head in each of his hands. There is a dog on his side who is believed to be his companion.

Another of Shiva's forms is Khandoba. This folk god appeared to rid the world of two demons, Malla and

Mani. Khandoba on his horse, accompanied by his wife Mhalsa also has his faithful dog for company. Defeated by the great Lord Khandoba, the demon Mani repented and sought forgiveness for the evil he had wrought. Malla, however, continued to seek the destruction of the universe even as he lay dying of the fatal wounds he had incurred in the battle with the god.

As a result of his repentance, Mani became a demigod who earned the god's pardon and benevolence, but the arrogant Malla suffered a different fate and came to a rather bloody end.

In order to stop the demon from his evil ways, an angry Khandoba killed him by taking off his head with a single blow. However, as blood spouted from his neck, the god grew worried as he knew that new demons would be born the moment a single drop of Malla's blood touched the ground.

Before he could think of a solution and before a new breed of terrible demons were born, Khandoba's faithful dog leapt to the scene and lapped up every single drop of blood that gushed from Malla's neck. Thus the world was saved from great evil by the quick thinking of this god's faithful Sarameya.

Apart from Lord Shiva, Lord Dattatreya, the incarnation of the supreme being representing Creation, Preservation and Destruction, or the holy trinity of Brahma, Vishnu and Shiva, is also associated with dogs. Although his earthly avatar is that of a sage, Dattatreya has powers that surpass those of the gods themselves. He is always shown dressed as a sage, carrying a *jhola*, or cloth bag, and followed by four dogs.

These four dogs are believed to be the earthly representations of the four Vedas, namely the Rig Veda, Yajur Veda, Sama Veda and Atharva Veda. Legend goes that the Vedas knew that they would lose all importance and be disregarded in the Kali Yuga and thus they assumed the form of dogs and went to Dattatreya, the supreme sage for protection. He blessed them with fearlessness and gave them his eternal protection. Thus these Sarameyas represent Dattatreya's mastery over the Vedas as well as his kindness and grace towards creatures, great and small.

MythNotes

One of the most popular rituals associated with Lord Bhairava takes place in Nepal. It is known as 'Kukur Tihar' and is observed during the months of early winter. People worship the dog as the companion of Bhairava. On this day, a red vermilion mark is applied on all dogs, and they are then garlanded and offered food. The ritual is a sort of a thanksgiving to dogs that guard homes and protect wealth, women and children.

There is a parallel story regarding the Pani incident through which Sarama, instead of being the saviour, was discredited and shamed. According to this version, Sarama was bribed by the Panis with a bowl of milk and when she returned to heaven, she lied to Lord Indra regarding the whereabouts of the cattle. Upon being cross-questioned she actually threw up some of the milk she had swallowed and ended up proving her guilt. This story discredits Sarama's contribution to the defeat of the Panis and is probably due to the lowering of dogs in the social hierarchy over time.

Some texts describe Sarama and her family as the 'dog-spirits' who cause coughs and colds in children. This is part of Lord Indra's gift to Sarama which gave her special powers. In order to ward her off, all mothers had to worship her with special prayers and offerings.